Wiggles and Squiggles

60 Bible-Based Classroom Games and Activities

By:
Vicki Boston,
Debbie Stroh, Judy Christian,
Diane J. Grebing, and Jane Elling Haas

CONCORDIA PUBLISHING HOUSE · SAINT LOUIS

This edition published in 2007 by Concordia Publishing House
3558 S. Jefferson Avenue
St. Louis, MO 63118-3968
1-800-325-3040 • www.cph.org

All rights reserved. Unless specifically noted, no part of this publication may be reproduced, stored in a retrieval system, or transmitted, in any form or by any means, electronic, mechanical, photocopying, recording, or otherwise, without the prior written permission of Concordia Publishing House.

The purchaser of this publication is allowed to reproduce the marked portions contained herein for use in the classroom and to send home for parents to use with children. These resources may not be transferred or copied to another user.

Unless otherwise indicated, Scripture quotations are taken from the HOLY BIBLE, NEW INTERNATIONAL VERSION®. NIV®. Copyright © 1973, 1978, 1984 by International Bible Society. Used by permission of Zondervan Publishing House. All rights reserved.

Scripture quotations marked KJV are from the King James or Authorized Version of the Bible.

Material in this book originally published in:

Christ's Kids Create 2 © 1993 Concordia Publishing House, pages 8, 9, 29

Kingdom Crafts for Kids © 1994 Concordia Publishing House, pages 8, 10

Operation Art © 1995 Concordia Publishing House, pages 12, 22, 30, 34

On Your Mark, Get Set, Create © 1996 Concordia Publishing House, pages 17, 32, 40, 52, 56–59, 62

Create-a-Treasure © 1997 Concordia Publishing House, pages 25, 31, 38, 54

Jungle Crafts for Kids © 1999 Concordia Publishing House, page 20

Outback Crafts for Kids © 2000, Concordia Publishing House, page 15

Mystery Crafts for Kids © 2001 Concordia Publishing House, page 21

Godzwerkus Circus School Craft Book © 2002 Concordia Publishing House, page 19

Ewe Can Craft! © 2003 Concordia Publishing House, page 16

Construct-a-Craft Craft Book © 2004 Concordia Publishing House, pages
6, 7, 10–12, 36, 37, 39, 40, 43, 46, 47, 49

Wild Safari Craft Book © 2005 Concordia Publishing House, pages 23, 24, 28

Stripe's Silly Games: Game Leader Guide © 2005 Concordia Publishing House, pages 6, 42, 45, 48, 50, 51, 53

Gem Games Leader Guide © 2006 Concordia Publishing House, pages 33, 35, 44, 55, 60, 61

Cover photo: © Magdalena Bujak/Shutterstock

Manufactured in the United States of America

1 2 3 4 5 6 7 8 9 10   16 15 14 13 12 11 10 09 08 07

contents

Introduction 5

Quiet Games

Creation Walk 6
Follow Me! 6
Hammer It 7
Invisible Memory Review 8
Pop-a-Prayer Pal 8
Team Memory Work 9
Thanksgiving Roll 10
Disappearing Act 10
Human Confusion 11
Pair Up 12
Decoder Wheel 13
Game Sticks 15

Board Games

Gather-the-Flock Game 16
Magnetic Maze 17
Smooth Stones Tick-Tac-Toe 19
Leap Frog 20
Mansion Checkers 21
Pebble Search 22
Tic-Tac-Tell Game 23
Bring-in-the-Harvest Game 24
"Forgiven Sins"
   Memory Game 25
Follow-the-Star Game 28

Active Classroom Games

Memory Relay	29
Bible Verse Discoveries	30
Logical Deductions	30
"Catch a Fish" Game	31
Giant Beanbag Throw	32
Jesus Loves Me	33
Can You Guess It?	34
Basket, Fish, and Bread	35
Builders' Challenge	36
Demolished but Rebuilt	37

Energetic Games

Fishing Game	38
Watch the Snake!	39
Horse Course	40
Winning Together, Working Together	40
Challenge Walk	42
Creation Scramble	43
Faithful Followers	44
Fishing for Men	45
Friendship Challenges	45
Get That Snake	46
Hit or Miss	47
Look Up and Go!	48
Sun, Moon, and Stars	49
Tree Tag	49
Faith Hurdles	50
Up Ball	51
Bible Bowling	52
Mat Mayhem	53
Journey Time Relay	54
Treasure Rescue	55
Bible Baseball	56
First Aid Relay	57
Toilet Tissue Wrap Relay	58
Tree Coin Toss	59
Wash Away Sins	60
Get-Me-Wet Shipwreck	61
Bubblelympics	62
Scripture Index	63

introduction

It happens in every classroom. Eventually, students grow weary of sitting and they start to wiggle. They grow weary of neat handwriting and they start to squiggle. What do you, their teacher, do to guide their energies and still help them learn? You introduce a game or activity that gets them on their feet.

This book offers 60 classroom games and activities that will be welcomed by any teacher or student. Each one reinforces Bible themes and concepts by connecting with a Bible verse or story. They are intended to help teach fundamental skills and give children a fun, creative outlet for the expression of their faith.

The games offered here are accomplished with simple and easily obtained materials. They are designed for a classroom with a tight budget and for teachers who are looking for creative ways to integrate faith into classroom activities. Each activity includes a materials list, instructions, and a Bible connection. Reproducible patterns are provided where appropriate. Some games or activities do require more adult assistance and are better suited for older children. Some are intended for use in the classroom and some are appropriate for large areas. And still others, because they involve water, should be played outdoors.

These games and activities have been chosen for their applicability to the Christian school. Use them as they are presented here, or use them to supplement your program. Feel free to adapt them as necessary to fit your students' interests and abilities.

May God's Spirit fill you with wisdom and joy as you share His love and mercy with the children in your care.

The Editors

Quiet Games

Creation Walk

Directions

Help the children hold hands and make a circle. While holding hands, walk in a circle and sing these words to the tune of "This Old Man":

**God made you. God made me.
He made the animals, plants, and trees,
Planets, stars, and sun shining bright.
Ev'rything God made was right!**

Explain to the children that God made the world and everything in it. He made animals, sea creatures, plants, people, everything! Ask one or two children to name something God made. Walk and sing again, repeating until each child has an opportunity to respond.

Bible Connection

In the beginning God created the heavens and the earth. Genesis 1:1

Creation

God's divine design perfectly reflected the creativity, love, power, and goodness of its Creator. He perfectly provided a prime environment for His creatures to prosper and grow. He gave Adam and Eve purposeful work, blessed them, and enjoyed them. Although sin destroyed this perfection, God promised to send One to restore His people. How wonderfully our good God kept this promise in Christ, our Savior!

Follow Me!

SUPPLIES
1 index card per person
Pen or marker

Directions

Make a set of cards. Draw a smiley face on all cards but one. Draw an X on the last card. Shuffle cards. Sit in a circle. Let each player choose a card, but not show it to anyone. Whoever receives the X card is the leader. Start a motion or rhythm everyone can follow, such as clapping, and have everyone join in. Then the leader will begin a new movement to the same rhythm. The leader might snap, tap a knee, touch his or her nose, or do something else. The group watches closely and changes to the new movement while trying to find and identify their leader. Reshuffle and play again.

Bible Connection

As Jesus was walking beside the Sea of Galilee, He saw two brothers, Simon called Peter and his brother Andrew. . . . "Come, follow Me," Jesus said, "and I will make you fishers of men." At once they left their nets and followed Him. Matthew 4:18–20

The calling of the first disciples

How can we follow Jesus when we cannot see Him? We follow Jesus when we learn about Him and hear His words in the Bible. Our church and families teach us about Jesus and His love for us. In thanks for all God has done for us in Jesus Christ, we want to find out what pleases Him. We want to follow Jesus, copy Him, and be like Him. We follow Jesus with joy and excitement!

Hammer it

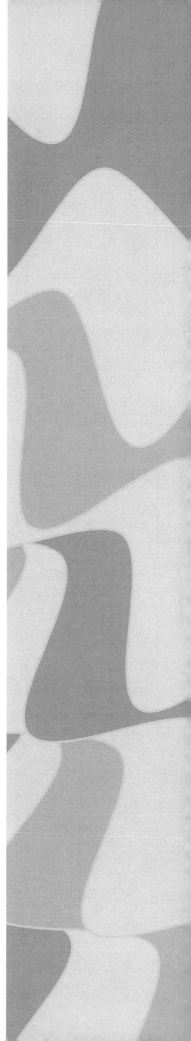

Directions

Help the children stand in a circle. Teach this song to the melody of "Did You Ever See a Lassie?" while you make a hammering motion with one fist.

All the workers had one hammer, one hammer, one hammer.
All the workers had one hammer; they hammered all day.
They hammered this way and that way, and this way and that way.
All the workers had one hammer and then they had two.

Sing the song again, but sing "two hammers" and "then they had three" while you hammer with both fists. Sing the song with "three hammers" while adding the motion of stomping one foot. Sing a final time with "four hammers" while hammering both fists and stomping both feet. Sing the last line as "and then they went home."

Bible Connection

Now the earth was corrupt in God's sight. . . . So God said to Noah, "I am going to put an end to all people. . . . But I will establish My covenant with you, and you will enter the ark." Genesis 6:11–13, 18

The flood

In Noah's time, God was grieved over the utter sinfulness of the world, so He sent a flood to wash the world clean. Only Noah and his family were still faithful to God. God spared them by instructing Noah to build an ark. God used a hammer to help us with our problem of sin. Jesus was nailed to the cross with a hammer and nails. He died to take away our sins. God repaired the world through Jesus.

Invisible Memory Review

SUPPLIES
White paper
Waxed paper
Magazine
Pencils
Bible

Directions

Instruct students to place a piece of waxed paper over a piece of white paper with a magazine under it. Write a favorite Bible verse or memory verse on the waxed paper. Press hard. Throw away the waxed paper. Have students exchange white pieces of paper with the person behind or beside them. Show students how to hold a pencil almost parallel to the paper. Lightly rub the pencil over the sheet of paper. Take turns reading one another's Bible verses.

Bible Connection

This activity can be used with any Bible story or verse. Consider using it with memory work. For example, if your class is studying the Apostles' Creed, each student could write a few words of the creed then exchange his or her paper with the student in front or behind.

Pop-a-Prayer Pal

SUPPLIES
Paper strips
Pen or pencil
5" balloons
Balloon sticks

Directions

Write each student's name on a strip of paper. Fold the paper and slip it into a balloon. Inflate each balloon, tie, and attach to a stick. Have each child choose a balloon and pop it. The paper inside gives the name of that student's prayer pal. They can pray for their pals throughout the school year or for a designated length of time.

Bible Connection
"Ask and it will be given to you; seek and you will find; knock and the door will be opened to you. For everyone who asks receives; he who seeks finds; and to him who knocks, the door will be opened."
Matthew 7:7–8

The Lord's Prayer

Prayer is a special gift from God. He invites us to come to Him in prayer and promises to hear us. Jesus gives us the model for prayer in Luke 11:1–4. Help students understand that there are many ways to pray and that we can pray wherever we are.

This activity can be used to supplement a unit on general prayer or on the Lord's Prayer. It makes a good first day of school ice breaker. Or it can be used for Special Friends Day, when older students are paired with younger students, if your school provides that program.

Sing "God, Our Father, Hear Your Children."

Team Memory Work

SUPPLIES
3" x 5" index cards
Scissors
Marker

Directions

Cut the index cards into fish, star, or heart shapes. Write one word of the memory verse on each card shape. Make two sets. Divide the class into two teams. Give each team one shuffled set of cards. Each team is to put the words in the correct order and display the whole verse on a chalkboard ledge or table for everyone to see.

Options: Give each person on the team one card. He or she must go forward at the correct time to place his or her word in correct sequence. Or have the children stand and hold their words in correct order.

Bible Connection
This activity can be used with any Bible verse or memory work assignment.

Thanksgiving Roll

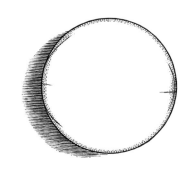

SUPPLIES
Playground ball

Directions

Seat the children on the floor in a large circle. Think of and then name things for which we are thankful. Roll the ball. The receiver says, "Thank You, God for _____." Continue until all have had a turn.

Bible Connection
Then Moses and the Israelites sang this song to the Lord: "I will sing to the Lord, for He is highly exalted." Exodus 15:1

The song of Moses' thanksgiving

After God delivered Moses and the children of Israel to safety through the waters of the Red Sea, they sang a song of thanksgiving to God. We sing a song of public thanksgiving every Sunday in the Service of the Word. This activity is a fun and simple way to remind children to offer their thanks to God at all times and places, for big things and for little things. We are especially thankful to God for delivering us through the wilderness of sin and into the kingdom of forgiveness and mercy through His Son, Jesus Christ.

Disappearing Act

Directions

Choose three to five players to leave the area and change three things about their appearance (e.g., trade glasses, pull down a sock, turn a T-shirt backward or inside out). When these players return, they should stand in front of the class for ten seconds. Then leave again. The players restore their original appearance then return to the classroom, standing in a different order than before. The rest of the class will try to place the players in their original order and identify the changes each person made. Repeat if you like.

Bible Connection
When He was at the table with them, He took bread, gave thanks, broke it and began to give it to them. Then their eyes were opened and they recognized Him, and He disappeared from their sight. They asked

each other, "Were not our hearts burning within us while He talked with us on the road and opened the Scriptures to us?" Luke 24:30–32

On the road to Emmaus

The disciples were with Jesus every day for three years. He clearly told them He would suffer, die, and rise again. Still, they did not understand. Two disciples discussed their confusion as they walked from Jerusalem to Emmaus on Easter morning. They mourned Jesus' death and wondered about His missing body. They failed to recognize Jesus when He joined them on the road. Only later, after He broke bread for a meal, did they finally recognize their Lord. Then He disappeared from their sight. We know that God's love for us will never disappear. He shows us this love in that He gave His Son to suffer and die for us, taking away our sins and restoring us to righteousness.

Human confusion

Directions

Sit with students in a circle on the floor. Begin by turning to the person on your right and saying, "This is my arm," while actually pointing to your head. The next person repeats the phrase and action, then adds another confused statement and action. Play continues around the circle until everyone adds an item. The faster you play, the more fun and challenging the game.

Bible Connection
For we do not have a high priest who is unable to sympathize with our weaknesses, but we have one who has been tempted in every way, just as we are—yet was without sin. Hebrews 4:15

Jesus, our high Priest

Sin brought death and confusion into the world, but remember that God made us and cares for us. God did not leave us alone or confused. He promised to send a Savior from sin, and He did it when He sent His very own Son, Jesus. Jesus lived as a human in our world, yet He never sinned. Although sin made us His enemies, Jesus died for us, paying for our sins on the cross. He acted as our high Priest by going before God on our behalf. God raised Jesus from the dead and, by grace through faith in Him, there is no confusion that Jesus covers our sins with His precious blood and makes us part of His Church.

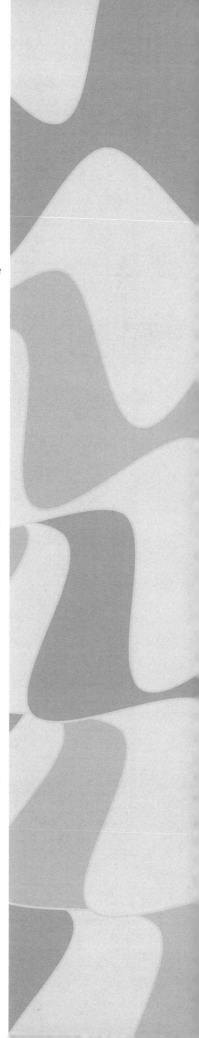

Pair Up

SUPPLIES
Self-stick notes
Markers

Directions

Write these words on self-stick notes, one per sheet: Adam, Eve, mom, dad, chicken, rooster, lion, lioness, bull, cow, buck, doe, drone, queen, gander, goose, stallion, mare.

Stick paper names to each person's back. Let participants move around, asking yes-or-no questions of other students until they have guessed the name on their back. Once they do, they need to find the student with the name that completes the pair. When they do, they sit by that person. The game ends when everyone is correctly paired.

Bible Connection
[Noah and his family] had with them every wild animal. . . . Pairs of all creatures that have the breath of life in them came to Noah and entered the ark. The animals going in were male and female of every living thing, as God had commanded Noah. Genesis 7:14–16

The flood

God created animals and people in pairs, male and female, so they could populate the world. When God created families, He designed a way for life to continue. And God continues to provide for us by giving us family and friends who care for us, provide a home for us, and show us love. Just like God showed care for Noah and his family by saving them from the flood, God shows His care for us by saving us through His Son, Jesus, our Redeemer and Savior!

Decoder Wheel

SUPPLIES
Card stock or old manila file folders
Compass
Pencils
Scissors
Brads
Bible
Index cards or paper

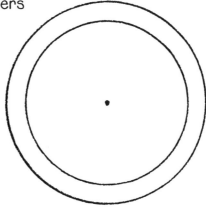

Illustration 1
5" circle

Directions

Use the compass to draw two circles (one 4", one 5") on the card stock or file folders for each student. Cut out the circles. Mark the center of each circle by making a small dot with a pencil. On the large circle, use a pencil to draw a light line 1 inch from the edge around the entire circle. On the inside of that line, write the letters of the alphabet in order, spacing the letters as evenly as possible. On the outside of the line, draw a symbol to represent each letter. **Note:** The symbol for each letter must be printed exactly across the circle from the letter it represents. Give younger students an established code to follow, perhaps the one illustrated. Older students can design their own code symbols or use the suggested one. Cut a small triangular notch out of the small circle as shown. The notch should be slightly larger than one of the letters so the letter will show from under the triangular cut. Affix the small circle on top of the large circle with a brad through the center of each circle. On the small circle, draw an arrow opposite the notched opening. See illustration 4.

To code a message, turn the small circle until the needed letter is in the triangular opening. The arrow will then point to the corresponding symbol. Copy a Bible verse using the symbols instead of letters. To decode a message, turn the arrow until it points to the symbol and the corresponding letter will appear in the opening.

Divide the students into pairs. Give each pair a Bible, several index cards or sheets of paper, pencils, and their decoder wheels. Invite them to look up Bible verses they have learned and write them down. Trade messages between pairs to decode. Print the decoded verses on the back of the cards or paper.

Bible Connection
The Lord continued to appear at Shiloh, and there He revealed Himself to Samuel through His Word. 1 Samuel 3:21

The Lord calls Samuel

God called to Samuel during the middle of the night when he was asleep. At first Samuel was confused and thought the voice came from the priest, Eli. We hear God speaking to us through His Word, the Bible, when we read Scripture and when we go to church and hear His Word proclaimed.

Use these decoder wheels to give your students practice time with Bible verses they have learned. Witnessing messages can also be devised and sent in code to share the Good News about Jesus with classmates and friends.

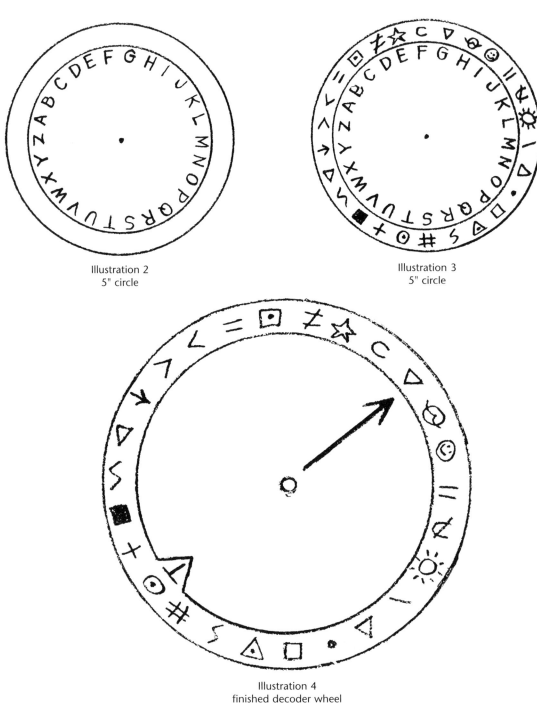

Illustration 2
5" circle

Illustration 3
5" circle

Illustration 4
finished decoder wheel

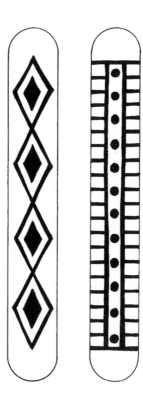

Game Sticks

SUPPLIES

6 or more large craft sticks
Acrylic paint
Paintbrushes
Cup of water
Paper towels or newspaper

Directions

Paint a different pattern or color on one side only of each craft stick. Let dry. Assign point values to each color or pattern and determine a total score that will indicate the winner. To play, hold the sticks about a foot above the floor or table, then drop them. Keep score for each student, counting only those sticks that land pattern- or color-side up. Take turns and see how long it takes to reach the score.

Bible Connection
Do you not know that in a race all the runners run, but only one gets the prize? Run in such a way as to get the prize. They [train] to get a crown that will not last; but we do it to get a crown that will last forever. 1 Corinthians 9:24–25

The best prize

We all like to win because that means we're the smartest, fastest, strongest, most accurate, etc. The downside of winning is, of course, losing. But Jesus makes us all winners! Jesus, our Lord and Savior, has saved us lost sinners and made us winners through His death and resurrection. The real prize is heaven, the eternal home Jesus has won for us.

Board Games

Gather-the-Flock Game

SUPPLIES
10 small round rocks
Acrylic paints
Paintbrush
Paper towels or newspaper
Cup of water
1 empty snack-size potato-chip can
Scissors
Construction paper
Markers
Glue stick
Small bouncy ball

Directions

Paint the rocks in bright colors; let dry. Paint a small sheep on each rock. Cut a piece of construction paper to fit around the can and decorate it. Glue the paper around the can.

To play, put the rocks in the can, shake the can, and spill out the rocks. Bounce the ball and pick up one stone before you catch the ball. On your next turn, bounce the ball, but this time pick up two stones before you catch the ball. Continue until you can pick up all ten stones before the ball bounces twice. Play with a friend by taking turns each time someone misses the ball.

Bible Connection
[Jesus] "came to seek and to save what was lost." Luke 19:10

The parable of the lost sheep

As you teach this Bible story and lead this activity, explain to students that when our first parents sinned, we became lost to God. Jesus came to take us back to God. When we were baptized, Jesus, the Good Shepherd, found and gathered us to Him and made us all members of His flock. Jesus loves each of us so much and never wants anyone to be lost from Him.

Magnetic Maze

SUPPLIES
Lamb and maze pattern
8 1/2" x 11" paper
Cardboard
Scissors
Cookie sheets
Transparent tape
White construction paper
Pencils
Paper clips
Small magnets

Directions

Duplicate one copy of the maze for each student on 8 1/2" x 11" paper. Older students could design their own mazes on 8 1/2" x 11" paper. Duplicate the lamb pattern. Make several lamb stencils on cardboard. Let the students use the lamb stencils to trace and cut their own lamb from white construction paper. Tape a paper clip to the back of each lamb.

Distribute the cookie sheets and mazes to the students. Tape the maze to the cookie sheet. Have the students place the lamb at the start of the maze. Give each student a small magnet. Show them how to place the magnet under the cookie sheet until it grabs onto the paper clip attached to the paper lamb. Invite the children to maneuver their lamb around the maze using the magnet until they reach Jesus, the Good Shepherd, at the end of the maze.

> *Bible Connection*
> *The LORD is my shepherd, I shall not be in want. He makes me lie down in green pastures, He leads me beside quiet waters, He restores my soul. He guides me in paths of righteousness for His name's sake. Psalm 23:1–3*

The Lord is my Shepherd
The parable of the lost sheep

Use this activity as you review Psalm 23 or the parable of the lost sheep with the students. As the children move their lambs around the maze, ask them to name the many things Jesus does for us as our Good Shepherd: He loves us, protects us from danger, provides for our needs, gives us eternal life. When students take their mazes home, encourage them to share these truths with family members as they guide the lamb through the maze to Jesus.

18

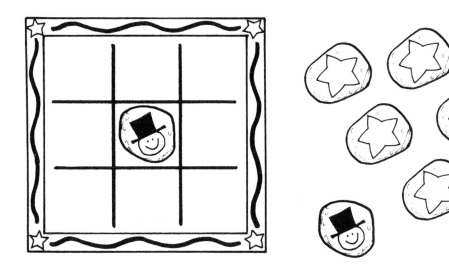

Smooth Stones Tic-Tac-Toe

SUPPLIES
9" x 9" piece of heavy cardboard or wood
Ruler
Pencil
Acrylic paints
Paintbrushes
Cup of water
Paper towels or newspaper
10 small smooth stones
Gallon-sized reclosable plastic bag

Directions

Draw a tic-tac-toe grid on cardboard or wood. Let dry. Divide stones into two sets. Paint each set to match. Distinguish sets by painting two different colors of stars or another simple design. Let dry. Place game pieces and game board in the plastic bag. Take along and play anywhere.

Bible Connection
[David] chose five smooth stones from the stream, put them in the pouch of his shepherd's bag and, with his sling in his hand, approached the Philistine. 1 Samuel 17:40

David and Goliath

With God's help, David defeated Goliath. The smooth stones of the tic-tac-toe game remind us of David's complete confidence in the Lord. God was with David all the days of His life. Rejoice that God is always with you too! We know this because God sent Jesus to defeat our enemies too—sin, death, and the devil.

Leap Frog

SUPPLIES

Foam core, 1/4" thick
   (available at hobby or art supply stores)
Pencil
Craft knife (adult-use only)
Small box with lid
Craft glue
Acrylic paints
Paintbrushes
Paper towels or newspaper
Cup of water
Hammer (adult-use only)
3-inch common nail
Dozen golf tees
Plastic jar lid

Directions

Prior to craft time, cut the foam core to fit the top of the box lid. Have students glue foam core place, then paint a frog on the foam core top. When the paint dries, use the pencil to mark off a 13-hole game grid. Start with a center row of three dots, spaced about one inch apart. Add a row of two dots on both sides of the first row. Finish with a row of three dots added to each side of the grid. Use the hammer to gently tap the nail through the foam core and the box lid where the dots are. Place golf tees in all but one of the holes.

To play, use one of the tees on the board to jump another tee and land in an empty hole. Remove jumped tee. Continue jumping until you have only one tee left. You may jump in any direction. Collect the jumped tees in the jar lid. Store the pegs and lid inside the box when you're not playing the game.

Option: Make a leap frog game for a neighbor or family member. When you give your gift, tell the person that Jesus loves him or her so much that He died and became alive for them!

Bible Connection
Then the LORD said to Moses, "Go to Pharaoh and say to him, 'This is what the LORD says: Let my people go, so that they may worship Me. If you refuse to let them go, I will plague your whole country with frogs.'"
Exodus 8:1–2

Moses and the ten plagues

Moses asked the pharaoh to release the children of Israel from slavery ten

times. Pharaoh refused nine times. Each time he did, God sent a plague upon Egypt. The plagues, which grew progressively worse, were meant to teach Pharaoh that God is in command. This Bible story teaches us what happens when hearts are hardened toward God, and reminds us to follow His will and not our own. Just like God fulfilled His promises to deliver the children of Israel out of Egypt and into the Promised Land, through Jesus, God keeps His promises to us and delivers us to heaven.

Mansion Checkers

SUPPLIES
24—1 1/2" unpainted birdhouses
   (available at hobby or art supply stores)
Acrylic paints
Paintbrushes
Cup of water
Newspaper or paper towels
Pattern (right)
12" x 12" piece of white poster board
Ruler
Pencil
Markers

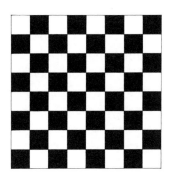

Directions

Paint twelve of the birdhouses with the same color and design to look like small mansions. Paint the other twelve with a contrasting color and design. Let dry. Draw a checkerboard, and using two contrasting color markers, fill in the squares according to the pattern.

Option: Enlarge pattern to make a 12-inch checkerboard. Move the completed birdhouses on the board as game pieces to play checkers. To "king" a mansion checker, turn the house backward or place it on its side.

Bible Connection
"In My Father's house are many mansions: if it were not so, I would have told you. I go to prepare a place for you." John 14:2 KJV

Jesus comforts His disciples

The disciples were troubled because Jesus had told them He would be going away and they couldn't go with Him. In this verse, Jesus offers comforting words—He is preparing a special place in heaven for them. This knowledge brings peace to the disciples and makes them secure in the promises Jesus extends to them. This Bible verse reminds us that we also have these promises. Jesus also makes a special place for us to be with Him in heaven one day.

Pebble Search

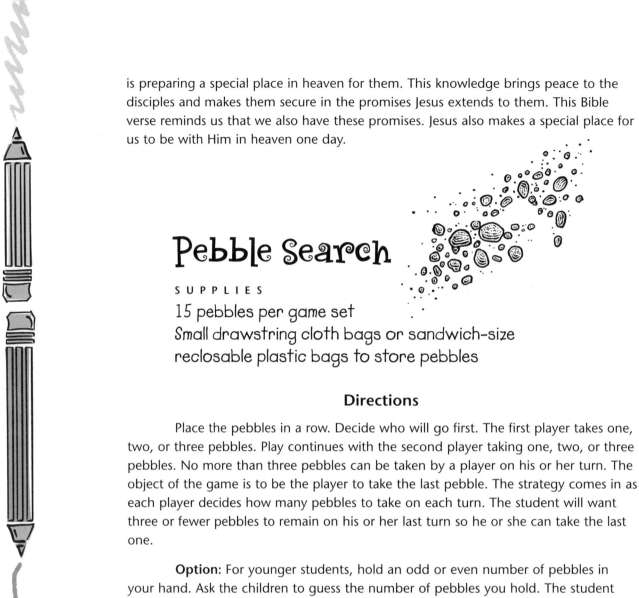

SUPPLIES
15 pebbles per game set
Small drawstring cloth bags or sandwich-size reclosable plastic bags to store pebbles

Directions

Place the pebbles in a row. Decide who will go first. The first player takes one, two, or three pebbles. Play continues with the second player taking one, two, or three pebbles. No more than three pebbles can be taken by a player on his or her turn. The object of the game is to be the player to take the last pebble. The strategy comes in as each player decides how many pebbles to take on each turn. The student will want three or fewer pebbles to remain on his or her last turn so he or she can take the last one.

Option: For younger students, hold an odd or even number of pebbles in your hand. Ask the children to guess the number of pebbles you hold. The student who guesses correctly gets to hold the pebbles for the next round.

Bible Connection
Jesus called the Twelve and said, "If anyone wants to be first, he must be the very last, and the servant of all." Mark 9:35

Who is the greatest?

We try to be the first because, in our culture, that means we're better. In this Bible verse, however, Jesus says it is better to serve others and to put them first. In the kingdom of God, we are all the same; we are all sinners. No one is better than anyone else. But Jesus served us—He took on our sin by suffering and dying on the cross. Jesus put us first and restored us to God. Christians show their faith in God by serving others.

Tic-Tac-Tell Game

SUPPLIES
11 jumbo craft sticks
Craft glue
Masking tape
Scissors
Paper towels or newspaper
Acrylic paint, various colors
Paintbrush
Cup of water
Pattern (right)
10 clean milk jug caps
Construction paper, yellow and green
Bible (optional)

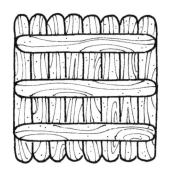

Directions

Place eight craft sticks side-by-side to form a square. To hold the sticks together, glue three craft sticks horizontally across the square as shown. Let dry. Turn the square over. Cut 4, 5 1/2-inch pieces of masking tape. Place them on the square to form the tic-tac-toe lines. Cover work area with newspaper. Paint the entire square playing surface with one color of acrylic paint. Let dry. Peel off the masking tape strips. Paint the lines of the tic-tac-toe grid a different color from the background. Let dry. Duplicate five crown patterns (enlarged) on yellow construction paper. Cut out and glue inside five milk jug caps. Duplicate five happy face patterns (enlarged) on green construction paper. Cut out and glue inside five milk jug caps.

Find a friend, select a playing piece, and play Tic-Tac-Tell (just like tic-tac-toe). The player who wins by getting three playing pieces in a row gets to share a fact about Jesus (from memory or the Bible) with the other player.

Bible Connection
But you will receive power when the Holy Spirit comes on you; and you will be my witnesses in Jerusalem and in all Judea and Samaria, and to the ends of the earth. Acts 1:8

Share the Good News about Jesus

Jesus sends us to tell others about Him. But we do not do it alone. The Holy Spirit helps us tell about Jesus, our Savior, wherever we are and whatever we do. Any time or place you are with a friend is a good time to share the Good News that Jesus is our Savior and King.

Bring-in-the-Harvest Game

SUPPLIES
2 egg cartons
Scissors
Tape
18 dry red beans
18 dry white beans

Directions

Thoroughly wash egg cartons. Cut off the lid from one carton. From another egg carton, cut off two single egg compartments. Tape one compartment to each end of the egg carton. Set up the game board. On one half of the egg carton, place three red beans in each compartment. On the other half of the egg carton, place three white beans in each compartment. Leave the single compartments on the end empty.

The object of the game is to get the most playing pieces in one's own storage bin. The single compartments at either end of the board are "storage bins." Players pick a side of the playing board.

Player one begins by taking all the pieces from any compartment on his or her side of the board. He or she then places one piece in each of the next three spaces, including, if necessary, his or her own storage bin. The player may place a piece in the compartments of player two's side, but not in player two's storage bin.

If a player's last piece lands in his or her own storage bin, that player takes another turn. If the last piece lands in a compartment, it is the next player's turn.

If the last piece lands in an empty space on his or her own side, that player can take the pieces from the compartment directly across and transfer them to his or her storage bin. If there are no pieces in the compartment, that player's turn is over.

The game ends when all the compartments on one side of the board are empty. The player whose side has empty compartments and the most pieces in his or her storage bin has won the game.

Bible Connection
Then He said to His disciples, "The harvest is plentiful, but the workers are few. Ask the Lord of the harvest, therefore, to send out workers into His harvest field." Matthew 9:37–38

The workers are few

Just as Jesus chose His disciples to become fishers of men, He also instructed His followers to bring a harvest of people into God's family. In the world, there are millions of people who do not know that Jesus is their Savior. Through Baptism, Jesus invites us to bring in the harvest so everyone everywhere can hear about His gift of salvation. We can share God's Word with others so they can believe that Jesus is their Lord.

When you play Bring-in-the-Harvest, think about the chances you have each day to tell other people about Jesus. Tell the other player about a time when God gave you an opportunity to bring in the harvest by sharing your faith in Jesus.

"Forgiven Sins" Memory Game

SUPPLIES
Copies of patterns on pages 26–27, 1 set per student
2 pieces of construction paper per student
Glue
Scissors
Markers or crayons
Picture of Jesus cut to fit grid
 (old Sunday School pictures work well)

Directions

Glue the number grid (page 26) to one side of a piece of construction paper. Trim it to fit. Glue the word grid (page 27) on the reverse side of the same sheet. **Note:** Make sure the grids line up with each other. Cut the squares apart. Set them aside. Glue the picture of Jesus to a piece of construction paper the same size as the grids.

Lay the picture of Jesus on the table. Place the numbered squares on top of the picture in numerical order from left to right, number-side-up. Two or more students can play. Play moves clockwise. The first player chooses two numbered cards. If the words under the numbers match, remove them and take another turn. If the words don't match, place them back on the board in their original positions. Help each other remember where words are hidden. Play ends when all cards are removed.

Options: Older students might design their own game pieces and pictures. Use different word grids to review Bible passages.

Bible Connection
So I say, live by the Spirit, and you will not gratify the desires of the sinful nature. Galatians 5:16

Life by the Spirit

When we say the Apostles' Creed, we say "I believe in the Holy Spirit, . . . the communion of saints." The Holy Spirit, the third Person of the holy Trinity, gives us the ability to believe and makes us part of the community of saints, or believers. On our own, we cannot believe. Through the work of the Holy Spirit, however, we come to faith in the triune God. When we believe, we want to obey God and serve Him—to "live by the Spirit"!

"Forgiven Sins" Memory Game Number Grid

1	2	3	4	5	6
7	8	9	10	11	12
13	14	15	16	17	18
19	20	21	22	23	24
25	26	27	28	29	30

"Forgiven Sins" Memory Game Word Grid

Pride	Gossip	Cursing	Anger	Envy	Jealousy
Arguing	Hatred	Judging others	Greed	Laziness	Pride
Laziness	Envy	Rebellion	Disobedience	Lying	Gossip
Judging others	Disobedience	Stealing	Arguing	Hatred	Anger
Lying	Jealousy	Cursing	Stealing	Greed	Rebellion

Follow-the-Star Game

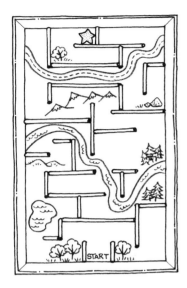

SUPPLIES
Drawing paper
Pencil
Scissors
1 shoe box lid
Markers
Light-colored construction paper
Craft glue
Star sticker
Chenille wire or plastic drinking straws
Marble

Directions

Cut a piece of drawing paper to fit the bottom of the inside of the shoe box lid. On the drawing paper, design a straight-lined maze pattern. Make sure there is only one way to get from one end of the shoe box lid to the other. Cut a piece of light-colored construction paper to fit the bottom of the inside of lid. Draw mountains, roads and other outdoor scenery on the paper. Glue paper in place. Lightly transfer the maze pattern from the drawing paper to the construction paper. Print "Start" at the beginning of the maze. Place a star sticker at the end of the maze. Cut chenille wire or drinking straws to glue over maze pattern. Glue the pieces to the pencil lines of the maze pattern. Let dry.

To play, place a marble at "Start." Maneuver the box lid so the marble travels to the star at the finish.

Bible Connection
After they had heard the king, they went on their way, and the star they had seen in the east went ahead of them until it stopped over the place where the child was. When they saw the star, they were overjoyed. Matthew 2:9–10

The visit of the Magi

Following a sign in the heavens, the Wise Men traveled a great distance and through what must have seemed like a maze of roads and routes until they found Jesus. They were overjoyed to find Jesus, their King. Jesus is our King. We don't have to follow a star or go through a maze to find Jesus. Through the Bible, the Holy Spirit leads us to Jesus and gives us faith in Him as our Savior and King.

Active Classroom Games

Memory Relay

SUPPLIES
Chalkboard
Chalk

Directions

Divide the class into two groups. Have them line up facing the chalkboard. The first person on each team goes to the board to write the first word of the memory verse. The second person writes the second word. Continue this until the whole verse is written by a team. Encourage the children to work as a group so all will feel successful.

Mix the children into different groups and repeat the activity.

Bible Connection

This activity can be used with any Bible story or verse. Consider using it with memory work for the week.

Bible Verse Discoveries

SUPPLIES

Chalkboard or large sheets of paper
Chalk or markers

Directions

Choose a Bible verse the children have been memorizing. Before the class session begins, print on the chalkboard or on large sheet of paper a Bible verse the students have studied, but leave out all the vowels. Where the vowels should be, leave blank lines. For older students, selected consonants also could be left out. Encourage the students, as they work in large or small groups, to fill in the missing letters to complete the verse. Use portions of the Apostles' Creed or the Lord's Prayer as well (if your students are familiar with them). This activity is another way students can review Bible verses and Christian truths using puzzle-solving skills.

Options: Teams could score points by taking turns at the chalkboard. When one team fills in all the *A*s (or the letter of their choice), they would score as many as they have found. Then the other team gets a turn. The team with the most points once the verse is complete wins.

You can also play this game in a "Wheel of Fortune" manner. Assign one point per vowel. If a team selects an E and there are eight in the puzzle, the team would be awarded eight points. The team with the most points when correctly guessing the verse wins.

Bible Connection

This activity can be used with any Bible story or verse. Consider using it with memory work for the week.

Logical Deductions

SUPPLIES
Card stock: green, yellow, blue, red
Marker
Chalkboard and chalk
Tape
Riddle
Clues
Bible, 1 per student

30

Directions

Create the six riddle cards before class using the correct colored card stock: Ephesians 2:8–9 (green); Matthew 22:37–39 (green); Isaiah 40:8 (yellow); Romans 5:8 (blue); Matthew 6:21 (red); Psalm 37:4 (green). Tape the cards to the chalkboard as you read the riddle. Have the class work together or in small groups to figure out the correct order.

Riddle

There are six Bible verses displayed on the bulletin board on colored cards: Ephesians 2:8–9; Matthew 22:37–39; Isaiah 40:8; Romans 5:8; Matthew 6:21; Psalm 37:4. These verses need to be put in order. Use the following clues and a Bible to place the verses in order on the board.

Clues

1. The verse about treasure and the verse about great commands are from the same book of the Bible but are not next to each other on the board and are not the same color.

2. The verse about flowers is below Matthew 6:21 and the verse on the blue card, but is above all the verses on green cards.

3. The longer Matthew verse is below one green card verse and Isaiah 40:8, but is above the verse that has the word *grace* in it.

4. The verse at the top is printed on a red card.

5. Psalm 37:4 is not next to the verse on the red card.

Answer

The correct order from top to bottom is Matthew 6:21, Romans 5:8, Isaiah 40:8, Psalm 37:4, Matthew 22:37–39, and Ephesians 2:8–9.

Bible Connection

This activity can be used with any Bible story or verse. To use this activity with memory work for the month, for example, have children keep a folder or binder of memory work, then write your own clues.

"Catch a Fish" Game

SUPPLIES
Medium-sized sponges, 3 for every 2 students
Pen
Scissors
Clean onion or potato bags, 1 for every 2 students

Directions

Cut the sponges into fish shapes. Divide the students into pairs. Give each pair a net bag and three sponge fish. One child holds the bag open while the other stands several feet away and tries to throw the sponges into it. Switch positions and repeat until each student has a turn.

Option: Adapt the activity by making other shapes such as doves, people, crosses.

Bible Connection
[Jesus] said, "Throw your net on the right side of the boat and you will find some [fish]." When they did, they were unable to haul the net in because of the large number of fish. John 21:6

The miraculous catch of fish

Use this game as a recreational activity after studying the Bible story. Make a set of game pieces for each student to take home. As they play with a parent, sibling, or friend, the child can retell the Bible story. Many of the people who followed Jesus, including some of His disciples, worked as fishermen. In this Bible story, the risen Jesus performed a miracle to teach Simon Peter—and us—that He had control over nature because He was God, the Son. In addition, Jesus makes us to be fishers of men. When we share our faith in Him, we "fish" for others and, by the power of the Holy Spirit, they come to faith in Jesus as our Savior.

Giant Beanbag Throw

SUPPLIES
Large cardboard appliance box
Goliath pattern (right)
Marker
Newspaper or paper towels
Acrylic paints
Paintbrush
Craft knife (adult-use only)
Masking tape
Beanbags

Directions

Before play begins, construct a giant beanbag throw board. Enlarge and trace the Goliath pattern as shown on page 32 to cover one side of the appliance box. Protect your work area with newspaper. Paint the drawing with colorful acrylic paints. Include point values as indicated on the pattern under each hole. When the paint is dry, use a craft knife to cut out the three holes as indicated on the pattern.

Make a masking-tape line at least 8 feet from the beanbag throw board. Give each student a beanbag. With toes behind the starting line, the players take turns trying to toss their beanbag into a hole. Any successful throw beats the giant.

Bible Connection
David said to [Goliath], "You come against me with sword and spear and javelin, but I come against you in the name of the L{\scriptsize ORD} Almighty." 1 Samuel 17:45

David and Goliath

David was an unlikely hero, but God helped him defeat the enemy of his people. Our greatest enemy is a giant—sin. Jesus defeated this giant when He died on the cross on our behalf. Because we have faith in Him, God protects us from our greatest enemy. Use this game in conjunction with the Bible story about David and Goliath. Each time a student makes a successful beanbag toss, ask him to name a time God protected him. Keep a list of the students' responses. When the game is over, thank God in prayer for all these instances of His protection.

Jesus Loves Me

SUPPLIES
Pencils
Half-sheets of paper
Heavy duty plastic spoons

Directions

Hand out paper and pencils. Have children write their names in large letters on the paper. Collect pencils. Then ask the group to sit in two lines facing each other, about 4 to 6 feet apart. Hand a spoon to each person. Have children crumple up the paper and use the spoon to shoot it at the other team. When each child gets someone's paper, have the child open it and say "Jesus loves _____," then read the name on the paper. Then shoot it back. Stop after about five minutes.

Bible Connection

"Therefore I tell you, do not worry about your life. . . . Look at the birds of the air; they do not sow or reap or store away in barns, and yet your heavenly Father feeds them. Are you not much more valuable than they? . . . But seek first His kingdom and His righteousness, and all these things will be given to you as well." Matthew 6:25–26, 33

Do not worry

God made the earth and all things in it. He started with nothing and turned it into something. He is in control! Sometimes we worry about things we can't control, such as what will happen in the future. But because we are God's children, He loves us and protects us. No matter what the future brings, we can be sure that God promises to save us from our sins and give us eternal life through Jesus.

can you guess it?

SUPPLIES
10 – 3" x 5" index cards
Pen
Large hat or shoe box

Directions

Before play, print the Ten Commandments, one per card, on the index cards. Place the completed cards into a large hat or shoe box. **Note:** If you have a large class, you may want to make more than one set of cards. Divide your class into two or more teams. A person from the first team will draw one of the commandment cards out of the hat or box. The team then has three minutes to work together to come up with a way to show their chosen commandment being followed in a positive way. No words can be spoken; only actions can be used. The team then presents their pantomime. The other team guesses which commandment is being acted out. The other team then has the chance to select a commandment and to pantomime it. Play continues back and forth between teams until all the commandments have been chosen.

Bible Connection

*Moses was there with the L*ord *forty days and forty nights without eating bread or drinking water. And he wrote on the tablets the words of the covenant—the Ten Commandments. Exodus 34:28*

The Ten Commandments

God gives us the Commandments to teach us how to behave toward Him and how to behave toward others. God's Law, the Commandments, are His way of setting direction and boundaries for us. He uses them to show us our sin and, therefore, our need for forgiveness. Sometimes we don't follow the Commandments very closely. We make mistakes. But because God loves us, He provides forgiveness for our sins through Jesus Christ, His Son. Jesus gave Himself for our sins and, because of this, we have the assurance of God's forgiveness.

Basket, Fish, and Bread

SUPPLIES
Newspaper or scrap paper
Sponges
Ink pen
Scissors
Baskets
Beach towels
Masking tape

Directions

Make paper wads to represent bread. Cut the sponges into fish shapes. Lay beach towels on the ground to mark the location of the river. Mark a starting line about 10 feet away from the river.

Divide the class into two or more teams, depending on class size. Give each team five paper wads, two fish, and one basket. Team members work together to move these items safely across river, but they will have a few challenges. Only one person at a time from each team can move an item. Each person can move only one item at a time. The basket cannot be left on the side with the bread alone. The bread can never be on a side without a fish. Once a team successfully moves all the items, the team may move to the other side of the river and sit down.

Let teams play and move their items with the limitations as listed. Remind students of the limits if you see a mistake, but let them work together to solve the challenges. Successful steps to move the items include: fish, bread, bread, bread, bread, bread, basket, fish; or fish, basket, bread, bread, bread, bread, bread, fish.

Options: For younger children, give only one challenge, that the basket can't be on one side with only the bread. For the youngest students, skip the challenges and simply ask them to move the items one at a time. Instead, the teacher may sit on the other side of the river and count items as they arrive (e.g., two fish, three bread, one basket). When done, ask students to say how many fish and loaves the boy gave to Jesus.

Bible Connection
Andrew . . . spoke up, "Here is a boy with five small barley loaves and two small fish, but how far will they go among so many?" John 6:8–9

Jesus feeds the 5,000

A boy with barley loaves and fish, comparable to five biscuits and two sardines, volunteered his lunch. Barley was the bread of the very poor, but the boy was rich in heart and willing to share. Jesus blessed the food and the disciples handed it out. Everyone ate his fill, and then the disciples filled twelve baskets with leftovers. How? Rich in love and compassion, Jesus, as God the Son, had command over nature and miraculously made a little go a long way. Later, His love for fallen mankind compelled Him to the cross to pay for our sins. Then He rose and now lives in heaven to give His love and riches to all who hear and believe.

Builders' challenge

SUPPLIES
20 or more small cardboard boxes
Masking tape or chalk

Directions

Mark an *X* in the center of your play area with masking tape or chalk. This is your building site. Pile the boxes 20 feet away. Point out the building site. Tell students that each one will get a chance to run to the site and add a brick to make a building project together. Have students line up and start the game. The first child grabs a "brick" and runs to the site to begin building. When that child returns, the next child goes to the site with a brick. Continue until the building collapses or the bricks run out. Challenge children to make taller or wider walls for the house.

Option: Challenge children to make specific things to illustrate other Bible stories such as the tower of Babel, Solomon's temple, or the well used by the Samaritan woman.

Bible Connection
"Everyone who hears these words of Mine and puts them into practice is like a wise man who built his house on the rock. The rain came down, the streams rose, and the winds blew and beat against that house; yet it did not fall, because it had its foundation on the rock." Matthew 7:24–25

The wise and foolish builders

God builds His Church with special materials. He doesn't use bricks to make His Church; He builds it with people who believe in Jesus as their Savior!

People often believe their accomplishments are the result of their own hard work or skills. But in truth, everything we have and do is the result of God-given gifts. When you teach this Bible story to older students, ask them to name things that might be similar to the foolish man's house (for example: an athlete who believes his or her success is the result of training, a successful self-made businessman). Explain that our talents, abilities, and skills are from God. Whatever we do with those talents is to be to the glory of God.

Demolished but Rebuilt

SUPPLIES
10 or more cardboard boxes (can be different sizes)
Large playground ball

Directions

Build a tower with the boxes. Line up students about 20 feet away from the box tower. Let the first person roll the ball to knock down the tower. If successful, let the roller quickly rebuild the tower. Continue playing until everyone has had a chance to roll the ball.

Bible Connection
By faith the walls of Jericho fell, after the people had marched around them for seven days. Hebrews 11:30

The fall of Jericho

Sin separates us from God. Jesus removed the sin that stood between us and God when He died on the cross and came alive again. Just as God knocked down the walls of Jericho for Joshua and the Israelites, Jesus knocked down the walls of our sins for us. Now we are no longer separated from God. Because of what Jesus did for us on the cross, God forgives our sins and fills us with His love! God's love makes us able to serve Him and help other people. We are His people, and He loves us.

Energetic Games

Fishing Game

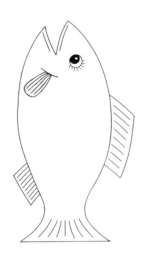

SUPPLIES
36" string
Small craft magnet
36" dowel
Thumbtack
Construction paper
Fish pattern (right)
Scissors
Pen or marker
Transparent tape
Small metal washers or paper clips
Large blue sheet or blanket
Poster board

Directions

For a small group, make one set of game items. For a large group, make a set for every four or five children. Make a fishing pole by tying a magnet to a string. Attach the other end to a dowel with a thumbtack. Cut out one construction-paper fish for each word in a Bible verse. Write one word on each fish. Attach a metal washer or paper clip to the back of each fish with tape. Place the fish on top of a blue sheet representing the Sea of Galilee. Play outdoors with a blue chalk lake drawn on the sidewalk.

On poster board, print the Bible verse reference and one blank for each word in it. As the children pick up fish, use tape to attach them to the blanks in the correct word order. Continue until the verse is completely filled in.

Options: For younger children, make a Bible story sequence game with one picture on each fish. Catch the fish and work together to put the pictures in the correct order. A story sequence game does not need the poster board prop. The children can simply lay the fish shapes on the floor in the correct order.

Make blank fish available and let older students create their own Bible verse puzzles to challenge their classmates.

Bible Connection

Andrew, Simon Peter's brother, was one of the two who heard what John had said and who had followed Jesus. The first thing Andrew did was to find his brother Simon and tell him, "We have found the Messiah" (that is, the Christ). And he brought him to Jesus.
John 1:40–42

Jesus' first disciples

Jesus often used fish and fishing as object lessons because His audience understood the parallels. Today's students may need a little more explanation. When teaching either of these Bible stories, begin by explaining how important fishing was to the people of Jesus' day so students will better understand the significance. Discuss what it means to be a "fisher of men" and have students list occasions or examples from their own lives when they can witness to their faith in Jesus as their Lord and Savior. Consider tying in a social studies or history lesson on the fishing industry or have students copy a map of the area.

Watch the Snake!

SUPPLIES
8 to 12' length of rope

Directions

Lay the rope in the center of the play area. Have children line up on one side of the rope. Explain that you will pretend the rope is a snake. You will move the rope, and when you yell, "Watch the snake!" children should leap over it without touching it. Kneel and hold one end of the rope, then shake it to slither like a snake. Afterward, ask students to name some things God gives us or does for us that show His love and care. Children may mention their families, homes, churches, friends, love, or other blessings from God.

> *Bible Connection*
> *So the LORD God said to the serpent, "Because you have done this, cursed are you above all the livestock and all the wild animals! . . . I will put enmity between you and the woman, and between your offspring and hers; He will crush your head, and you will strike His heel."*
> *Genesis 3:14–15*

God promises a Savior

Although Adam and Eve sinned and did what the devil wanted them to do, God still loved them. God cared for Adam and Eve by giving them clothing to wear and, more important, by promising to send a Savior to help them deal with the consequences of sin. God made us and cares for us too. That's why God sent Jesus as our Savior. Jesus died and rose from the dead to save all of us from our sin!

Horse course

SUPPLIES

3 plastic gallon buckets

Directions

In a grassy play area or gym, mark a triangle course with the buckets. Gather students by one bucket. Invite them to pretend to be horses and demonstrate different horse motions with you—walk, trot, gallop, graze, run, jump. Show the children how they will run around the outside of the triangle marked by the buckets. When ready, start several (or all) horses on the course. If you have everyone go together, run with them. Name different motions as children run, changing often and mixing fast and slow actions. If you like, have horses jump over buckets.

Bible Connection

Philip ran up to the chariot and heard the man reading Isaiah the prophet. "Do you understand what you are reading?" Philip asked. "How can I," he said, "unless someone explains it to me?" So he invited Philip to come up and sit with him. Acts 8:30–31

Philip and the Ethiopian

Philip was a Greek-speaking Jewish Christian and evangelist from Jerusalem. When persecution scattered the Christians, Philip preached the Word wherever he went. God sent Philip to share the story of Jesus Christ with an Ethiopian man who had traveled to worship in Jerusalem. Like Philip, God wants us to share the Word of God with others. By grace through faith in Jesus, God makes us part of His Church.

Winning Together, Working Together

SUPPLIES

Latex balloons (a different color for each small group—4 students per group, each person with the same color of balloon)
Heart-shaped balloons, 1 for each group
Several large drawstring plastic trash bags
Bendable metal coat hangers, 1 per student

Knee-high nylon stockings, 1 per student
Twist ties, 1 per student
Needle-nose pliers

Directions

Before class time, inflate and tie a latex balloon for each student (fill some extra balloons in case some burst). You will need to inflate four balloons of each color, one for each student in each group. Inflate and tie one heart-shaped balloon for each small group. Place the inflated balloons in several drawstring plastic trash bags for safekeeping until needed.

Have the students make racquets. Give each student a metal coat hanger. As illustrated, have each student pull down the long bottom side of the hanger to form a diamond shape. Help each student as necessary to slide a knee-high nylon stocking over the body of the hanger. Pull the open end of the stocking up to the top of the hanger and secure it with a twist tie. Bend down the curved end of the hanger so no sharp point exists. This will form a handle for the racquet. Have an adult use pliers to do this if necessary. **Note:** If you are doing this activity with four- or five-year-old students, make these racquets yourself before class begins.

Clear a large area of your classroom so there are no obstacles. Divide the class into groups of four. Distribute the inflated balloons to the students, with students in each group having the same color. Show the class how to gently tap the balloon with the center of the racquet to keep it afloat. Let each student practice this for a few moments. Be sure the students are a safe distance from one another so no one is hit with a racquet.

The object of the game is for everyone in each group to keep his or her balloon afloat. If a student sees a group member's balloon coming his or her way, he or she should try to keep the group member's balloon afloat as well as his or her own. Let the students enjoy doing this for several minutes.

Now add a heart-shaped balloon to each group's set of balloons. Tell the students that this balloon reminds us of Jesus' love for us. Tell the students to work together to keep not only their own balloons afloat but the heart-shaped balloon as well.

Bible Connection
*Before the spies lay down for the night, she went up on the roof and said to them, "I know that the L*ORD *has given this land to you. . . . Please swear to me by the L*ORD *that you will show kindness to my family, because I have shown kindness to you." Joshua 2:8–12*

Rahab and the spies

Rahab agreed to hide Israelite spies in exchange for protection for herself and her family. As a believer in God, she knew He had previously protected the children of

Israel and she hoped to have similar protection. Rahab tied a red cord in her window to lower the spies to safety. In the early church, this red cord was a symbol of Christ's blood and the love He poured out for us on the cross.

Before and after playing this game, remind the students that Jesus' love and His death for us as our Savior bring us together as members of God's winning team. Jesus' love motivates us to share this love with others. Jesus' love helps us work together as a team. In order for this balloon game to be successful, the students have to work together and help one another.

Challenge Walk

SUPPLIES
Masking tape
Objects to make an obstacle course, such as a balance beam, risers, chairs, tables, boxes
1 medium-sized box for every 4 to 6 participants
2 to 3 medium-sized rocks per box

Directions

Use masking tape to mark a path on the floor. Add wide places, narrow places, sharp turns, and other maneuvers so the path is challenging. Add other obstacles, such as risers or a balance beam. Group chairs and boxes to block a path or hide the view before a turn. If you have more than twenty children together at a time, set up more than one course.

Have students line up at the beginning of the obstacle course. Give the first person a box with two or more rocks in it. When this person is about one-quarter of the way into the course, let another person start. Continue so three or four people are in the course at a time.

When everyone has walked the course, challenge students to walk the course again, this time without carrying the rocks in the boxes.

Bible Connection
As they led Him away, they seized Simon from Cyrene, who was on his way in from the country, and put the cross on him and made him carry it behind Jesus. Luke 23:26

The crucifixion

Sin brings guilt, pain, misunderstanding, and hurt that makes life difficult for us and for others. It weighs us down and separates us from God and other people. Jesus died and rose for us to take the weight of our sins on Himself. Jesus paid for our sins on the cross! Everyone who believes in Jesus as their Savior receives forgiveness of sin and the promise of eternal life. Free from the weight of our sin, we can joyfully serve Jesus! This activity is designed to show students that we can walk through life burdened by sin or we can go through life knowing the freedom that forgiveness in Christ gives us.

creation scramble

SUPPLIES
Index cards, 1 per person plus a few extras

Directions

On cards, write names for or draw pictures of things God created (e.g., trees, flowers, elephants, stars). Make two cards for each item. Write a list of items on an extra card and keep separate. Shuffle the cards.

Have the students stand in a large circle with about 3 feet between participants. Give a card to every child except one, who stands outside the circle as a caller. Give this child the card with the list. When the child calls out an item on the list, the children with those two cards exchange places in the circle. As they do, the caller tries to reach one of the spaces first. The person who does not get a space becomes the new caller. The previous caller gets the new caller's card and place in the circle. Continue playing until everyone has been a caller.

Bible Connection
God saw all that He had made, and it was very good. Genesis 1:31

Creation

God made the world and everything in it. Everything God made, including each of us, has a special place in His creation. Everything God made is good and reflects His love for us. This love is shown in no greater way than in the work of Jesus in our lives. Although we sin, Jesus loves us and forgives us, making things right in the world again.

Faithful Followers

SUPPLIES
Dot stickers in 2 or 3 colors
Scissors

Directions

Cut apart dot stickers. Divide class into groups of six. Give each person three stickers. Make sure you vary the colors. Have students place each sticker on a hand or foot. Call out two colors. Students then connect the correct colors to both neighbors. For example, if you said, "Blue to yellow," a student could touch his blue hand dot to his neighbor's yellow foot dot, and his blue foot dot to his other neighbor's yellow foot dot.

When calling out colors, start giving directions slowly, then go faster as students get quicker at this task.

Options: Give each person a different colored dot to add to their forehead or fourth limb. Make a hand or foot part of your instructions. For example, say "touch a blue foot dot to a yellow hand dot." Groups will probably be able to do this only if they connect across the circle instead of with neighbors. But don't tell them this; let them figure it out. For younger children, use two dots each and limit them to either hands or feet.

Bible Connection
When they had gone, an angel of the Lord appeared to Joseph in a dream. "Get up," he said, "take the child and His mother and escape to Egypt. Stay there until I tell you." . . . So he got up, took the child and His mother during the night and left for Egypt. Matthew 2:13–18

The escape to Egypt

Joseph faithfully followed God's instructions. How can we continue to learn about God and follow Him? To learn about Him we need to read and understand God's Word, the Bible. The Bible is a treasure God gives us so we can know about Him, and about our Savior, Jesus. Where can we continue to learn about Jesus? Encourage students to continue learning about God's love for them in Jesus by attending Sunday School, worship, and other church activities. Encourage them to read the Bible and pray with their family members, spend time with Christian friends, and tell others about Jesus.

Fishing for Men

SUPPLIES

Something to designate or mark start and finish lines, about 100 feet apart

Directions

Choose one person to be a fisherman. Have the fisherman stand with his or her back turned toward the finish line. Have everyone else ("fish") line up on the starting line, facing the fisherman.

Help the fisherman learn and say this rhyme: "Fishes, fishes in the sea. Fishes with (color) on can't escape me!" When done, the fisherman turns around and any fish wearing the named color try to run to the finish line without being tagged by the fisherman. If caught, a fish becomes a fisherman and helps catch more fish in the next round. Play continues until all become fisherman. The last fish becomes the fisherman in the next round of play.

Bible Connection

Jesus said to Simon, "Don't be afraid; from now on you will catch men." So they pulled their boats up on shore, left everything and followed Him. Luke 5:10–11

Fishers of men

Jesus chose Simon to follow Him. Jesus chooses us to follow Him too. He calls us through His Word and makes us His children through the water and Word of Holy Baptism. Jesus came to find and save sinners. He did this by living without sin, but dying on the cross to pay for our sins. Jesus chooses us because He loves us. We show that we follow Him by worshiping Him, by studying what He says to us in the Bible, by praying to Him, and by sharing our faith in Him with others.

Friendship challenges

SUPPLIES

1 Frisbee for every 2 players
1 Hula Hoop for every 2 players
20 medium-sized boxes

Directions

Ask students to choose a partner. Give each pair a Frisbee. Then complete two or more of these challenges:

Challenge pairs to see who can complete a pass while standing the farthest apart. To begin, have groups stand 3 feet apart and toss the Frisbee. Each time pairs successfully catch the Frisbee, partners take one step backward, then toss it again.

Challenge pairs to see who can complete the most successive Frisbee passes. Stand pairs about 15 to 20 feet apart.

Challenge pairs to see how many times they can throw the Frisbee through a Hula Hoop in two minutes. While one tosses, the other holds the hoop above his or her head.

Set boxes 15 to 25 feet from a starting line. Stack some boxes so they sit at varying heights. Challenge pairs to get as many Frisbees in the boxes as they can in two or three minutes.

Bible Connection

Jonathan said to David, "Go in peace, for we have sworn friendship with each other in the name of the LORD." 1 Samuel 20:42

David and Jonathan

Even in Bible times, friends enjoyed playing games together. Because they were good friends, David and Jonathan probably did the same. When David's life was threatened, Jonathan came to his aid and protected him. Good friends are wonderful gifts God gives us during our lives here on earth. Jesus tells us what it means to be His friend: "Greater love has no one than this, that he lay down his life for his friends. You are My friends if you do what I command. I no longer call you servants, because a servant does not know his master's business. Instead, I have called you friends, for everything that I learned from My Father I have made known to you" (John 13:13–15). Jesus is our best Friend because He laid down His life for us and forgave our sins.

Get That Snake

SUPPLIES
Under-inflated playground ball

Directions

Stand in a circle with about 6 feet between participants. Select five to six players to make a snake by standing in a line in the center with their arms around the waist of the player in front of them. Give the ball to a person in the circle. Players roll the ball, trying to hit the last person in the snake. The snake continually moves and turns to avoid the ball. When hit, the last person takes the place of the roller. The roller becomes the head of the snake.

Bible Connection

Now the serpent was more crafty than any of the wild animals the LORD God had made. He said to the woman, "Did God really say, 'You must not eat from any tree in the garden'?" Genesis 3:1

The fall of man

Whether it's a serpent in the Garden of Eden or it's a modern day distraction, Satan takes on many forms and uses many arguments to weaken our faith and separate us from God. But we can resist the devil and all his ways. God loves us so much that He sent His Son, Jesus, to fight and defeat the devil for us! Jesus did this when He lived without sin and then died on the cross to pay for our sins. Jesus rose from the dead, defeating sin, death, and the devil forever!

Hit or Miss

SUPPLIES
Laundry baskets, 1 for every 5 students
Socks, 5 for every student

Directions

Roll socks into balls. Put the basket in the center of the play area. Have students try to shoot balls into the basket. Challenge players to hit the basket most often or from the farthest distance.

Bible Connection

Let us fix our eyes on Jesus, the author and perfecter of our faith, who for the joy set before Him endured the cross, scorning its shame, and sat down at the right hand of the throne of God. Hebrews 12:2

Staying focused

Sin causes us to miss the target, but remember that God made us and cares for us. God kept His promise to send us a Savior from our sin when Jesus was born, lived, and died on our behalf. God gave us His very own Son, Jesus. Through faith, we can stay focused on Jesus and His work in our lives.

Look Up and Go!

SUPPLIES
Yellow balloons, 1 each plus a few extras
Permanent marker
Large garbage bags (not black)
Chalk, masking tape, or string

Directions

Draw a star on each balloon. Inflate and tie securely. Write "King's House" on the garbage bags. Place inflated balloons in the bags. Define a small play area with about 30 square feet per player. Define the play area with chalk, masking tape, or string.

Scatter Wise Men (students) across the play area. Give each an inflated balloon. Tell Wise Men to walk and tap their balloons into the air while looking up.

Watch carefully and if a Wise Man comes within 5 feet of another person, yell out "I see a camel!" The two players must become a camel by linking arms and walking together, while continuing to tap their balloons and look up. If another person comes within 5 feet of a camel, he or she also links arms and joins in.

If a balloon belonging to a camel falls, everyone becomes Wise Men again. If no one becomes a camel, make your play area smaller.

At the end of the game, hold open a garbage bag. Challenge Wise Men and camels to tap their stars (balloons) into the "King's House" bag.

Bible Connection
Magi from the east came to Jerusalem and asked, "Where is the one who has been born king of the Jews? We saw His star in the east and have come to worship Him." Matthew 2:2

The visit of the Magi

Why did the Wise Men want to find Jesus? The Wise Men knew that God had promised to send a special King and Savior to His people. When Jesus was born, they saw the sign in the sky and knew that God had kept His promise of a Savior. They came to worship Jesus, God's own Son. Their worship of the child-king shows that they believed He was no ordinary mortal. They were right! Jesus is our King, God's Son, the Promised One who would redeem sinners with His death on the cross.

Wise men still seek the King. And so do wise women and wise kids. Share God's Word today so children may become "wise for salvation through faith in Christ Jesus" (2 Timothy 3:15).

Sun, Moon, and Stars

SUPPLIES
Masking tape, chalk, or yarn

Directions

Tape, draw, or mark a long line down the center of the play area. Either you can be the leader or you can have students take turns being the leader. Have students line up on one side of the line. If the leader calls "sun," the children jump to the other side of the line. If the leader says "moon," the students jump up and down three times. If the leader calls "stars," the children straddle the line. If the leader says the same name twice (sun, sun) students do not move. Call items faster to make the game more fun and challenging.

Bible Connection
God made two great lights—the greater light to govern the day and the lesser light to govern the night. He also made the stars. God set them in the expanse of the sky to give light on the earth, to govern the day and the night, and to separate light from darkness. And God saw that it was good. Genesis 1:16–18

The fourth day of creation

God made the world and everything in it just by speaking the words. Because He is God, He can make anything happen. Because God loves us, He made the sun, the moon, and the stars! And because God loves us, He made it possible for us to be His children. Our first parents, Adam and Eve, brought sin into the world by disobeying God. But through Baptism into Christ, God forgives our sin and gives us the promise of the perfect kingdom He created.

Tree Tag

Directions

Define boundaries for safe areas in a large play area. Select one student to be "It." Students run from one safe area to another, trying to avoid being tagged by "It". When tagged, students stand frozen with arms outstretched to look like a tree. Trees become runners again when tagged by other runners. Change who is "It" frequently.

Bible Connection
[Zacchaeus] wanted to see who Jesus was, but being a short man he could not, because of the crowd. So he ran ahead and climbed a sycamore-fig tree to see Him, since Jesus was coming that way. Luke 19:3–4

Zacchaeus the tax collector

It was not proper or easy for a rich, well-dressed man to scramble up a tree, but Zacchaeus did it. Zacchaeus had probably heard about Jesus' miracles or discussions with the religious teachers. He might have heard about Jesus' kindness to other tax collectors and sinners. Was this the long-promised Messiah? Zacchaeus had to see!

Zacchaeus saw Jesus and Jesus saw him too. He said, "Zacchaeus, come down immediately. I must stay at your house today" (Luke 19:5). Every sinner longs to hear these words! We yearn for Jesus to come and spend time with us.

Jesus came to earth because He wants a relationship with us. To make this possible, Jesus lived without sin, then willingly died on the cross and rose from the dead to pay for our sins. Everyone who believes in Jesus receives the benefits of His sacrifice—forgiveness of sin and eternal life. Our trees remind us that Jesus saved Zacchaeus. Jesus died on a tree to save us and take away our sins!

Faith Hurdles

SUPPLIES
Masking tape

Directions

Outdoors, on a paved surface, or in a gym, tape a series of masking tape lines of different widths. Lay the lines out as if on an obstacle course. Line up students at the beginning of the course. The first time through the course, have kids walk and jump over each hurdle (line) without touching the tape. The second time, have a different person be the lead. This time, run the course and jump each hurdle. On successive times, choose new leaders and skip, crawl, or hop without touching the lines.

Bible Connection
Then Jesus told him, "Because you have seen Me, you have believed; blessed are those who have not seen and yet have believed."
John 20:29

Jesus appears to Thomas

After Jesus' resurrection, the scars on His side, hands, and feet from His crucifixion gave physical proof of His identity. For some of Jesus' followers, there was a hurdle to their acceptance of His resurrection. For example, Thomas demanded proof. He needed to see and touch these scars before he would believe. When Jesus showed His scars, Thomas acknowledged Jesus' identity and role in his life—"My Lord and my God!" (John 20:28).

We are all special to God. Jesus showed us just how special by dying on the cross to take away our sins. Our sins are hurdles to our relationship with God. To take away these hurdles, Jesus died for our sins and rose from the dead. Now we have new life, now and forever. Jesus cares for us every day. He gives us many good gifts, including a home and people who love us, a beautiful world to live in, friends, and a church where we can learn about Him. In all of these ways and more, Jesus shows proof of His love for us.

Up Ball

SUPPLIES
Sidewalk chalk or masking tape
Playground balls

Directions

On pavement or sidewalk outdoors, use sidewalk chalk to draw a grid of eight squares, about 3 feet each. In six squares, write "Up." In two squares, write "Pass." (If you play this game indoors, use masking tape to mark floor.)

Players stand outside the grid and bounce the ball into a square. If the ball lands in a square labeled "Up," the player who receives the ball must name something that goes up or that you have to look up to see. Player must catch the ball before it bounces again. Players will learn to bounce the ball hard so they have enough time to think and catch the ball before it bounces a second time. If the ball lands in a square labeled "pass," the player catches the ball before the second bounce and bounces it to a new player.

Possible "Up" items include helium balloons, hot air balloons, stars, moon, sun, planets, angel who announced the birth of Jesus, the Epiphany star, the paralyzed man whom Jesus healed, Jesus rising from the dead, Jesus ascending to heaven.

Bible Connection
[Jesus] was taken up before their very eyes, and a cloud hid Him from their sight. Acts 1:9

Jesus ascends to heaven

Where is heaven? The Bible tells us that it is up. After Easter, the resurrected Christ spent another forty days on earth teaching His disciples about what to expect in the future and how they should minister to people. On Ascension Day, Jesus returned to heaven, going up into the sky on clouds. He is there still, at God's right hand. This Bible story also tells us that on the Last Day, Jesus will return to earth the same way. As Christians, we are encouraged to always be ready for Jesus' return.

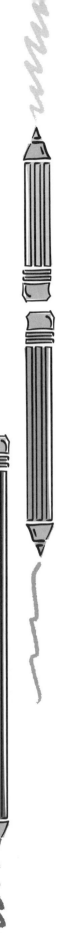

Bible Bowling

SUPPLIES
10 clear plastic two-liter soda bottles (labels removed)
10 (or more) white self-adhesive labels, name tag size
Marking pens
Masking tape
Small playground ball

Directions

Before play begins, place a label on the same place on each bottle. Choose a Bible verse to review. Print one word or a short phrase from the verse on each bottle label. Then line up the bottles in a row so the verse reads from left to right. Make a masking-tape line 8 feet from the bottles. (Shorten or lengthen this distance to accommodate the age of your students.) Have the students use a small playground ball to bowl the bottles down in the correct order, repeating the verse as they do. They should stay behind the masking-tape line as they bowl.

Bible Connection

This activity can be used with any Bible story or verse. Consider using it with memory work for the week.

Mat Mayhem

SUPPLIES
1 beach towel per group
1 laundry basket per group
4 stuffed animals per group
1 stopwatch

Directions

Mark a starting line. Place the laundry basket (hospital) about 50 feet away. Divide students into teams of four and give each team a beach towel (mat). Have each player grab a corner of the towel and gently pull until it's taut. Place a stuffed animal in the center of each towel. Line up teams behind a starting line. Teams are to carry the animal on their mat to the hospital, place it inside, and then return to the get another animal. If an animal drops, the group has to go back to the starting line and begin again. Play continues until all animals are in the basket. Time how long it takes for the team to complete the task. Play again, challenging teams to improve their transport times.

Bible Connection
Some men came, bringing to Him a paralytic, carried by four of them. Since they could not get him to Jesus because of the crowd, they made an opening in the roof above Jesus and, after digging through it, lowered the mat the paralyzed man was lying on. When Jesus saw their faith, He said to the paralytic, "Son, your sins are forgiven."
Mark 2:3–5

Jesus heals the paralyzed man

Word about Jesus had spread, so when He traveled from place to place, large crowds of people came to hear what He had to say. At a house in Capernaum, so many people gathered there was no room for anyone else. There were four men who were certain Jesus could help their friend, who was paralyzed. They were so certain that they made a hole in the roof of the house and lowered their friend down through the roof right in front of Jesus. Jesus healed the paralyzed man—but first He forgave the man's sins.

Two things happened in this Bible story to show that Jesus was God the Son. First, He forgave the man's sins—forgiveness comes from God. Second, He miraculously healed the man's body—miracles also come from God. Everyone who was there was amazed. We still receive forgiveness and healing through Jesus' work in the Word of God and in the Sacraments. This is amazing!

Journey Time Relay

SUPPLIES

Bedsheet piece, 3' x 6'
Cotton rope, 48" long
Adult-size slip-on sandals
Cotton drawstring laundry bags, stuffed with newspaper
Large knee-high socks
Plastic cone or something to mark the destination

Directions

Set up cone to mark the "destination." Divide students into teams of five and line them up behind a pile of items, one set of items for every team. When the teams are ready, demonstrate how to put on each item of clothing: The bed sheet slips around your shoulders to make a cloak. The rope is tied around your waist as a belt. The socks and sandals slip onto your feet. The laundry bag is slung across your back as a traveler's pack.

Tell students that when the time came for Moses and the Israelites to leave Egypt, they had to get dressed and leave quickly. Students are to pretend they are Israelites getting ready to follow Moses out of Egypt. Each person in line will take a turn putting on the traveling clothes. As soon as they have everything on they will go to the cone "destination" and return to take the items off as fast as possible and give them to the next person in line, who will dress and undress the same way. The player then goes to the back of the line. The first team to have every team member dress and undress in the travel clothes will win. They are allowed to help each other to avoid becoming entangled in the clothing.

Bible Connection

During the night Pharaoh summoned Moses and Aaron and said, "Up! Leave my people, you and the Israelites! Go, worship the LORD as you have requested. Take your flocks and herds, as you have said, and go."
Exodus 12:31–32

The exodus

The story of the ten plagues of Egypt helps us to remember what happens when hearts are hardened against God. Although Pharaoh asked Aaron and Moses to plead to the Lord on his behalf when things got rough, when the Lord lifted each plague, Pharaoh was back to his old ways. He refused to change. How often do we do the same? How often do we ask things of God, promising to do something in return then don't do what we promised? This story reminds us to follow God's wishes and not our own. We should remember the devotion of Moses and how he kept doing what the Lord asked even though it seemed like the Israelites would never be free as God had promised. The Israelites were kept safe from the dangers of the plagues and God gave them strength to endure their slavery until they were set free. This story offers a great opportunity to remind students that God keeps His promises and protects those that love Him.

Treasure Rescue

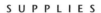

SUPPLIES
Small "treasures" (rolled-up socks, sponges, bean bags, paper wads, or pebbles)
Masking tape

Directions

Define and mark off a rectangular play area, about 60 feet by 40 feet. Mark a centerline. Mark treasure chest areas in diagonal corners.

Divide the class into two teams of equal size. Have each team stand on opposite sides of the centerline in their respective territories. They are safe from being tagged when they are on their side of the field. Give each student a treasure and have him place it in the other team's treasure chest, then return to his side. The object of the game is for each person to rescue his or her own treasure from the other team's treasure chest (in the diagonal corners) and return to their side without being tagged. Students may rescue only their own treasure, not anyone else's.

If a member of the one team tags someone on the opposite team, he becomes their treasure and stands in their treasure chest. A member of his team can rescue him by grabbing her own treasure and his hand. Then the two can walk back to their side without being tagged. Team members can rescue their treasure without rescuing other team members, but they are not safe to go back to their side.

Option: For younger students, simplify the game by making treasure chests go along the entire length of the end lines. Make the play area smaller. Let students rescue any person's treasure, not just their own.

Bible Connection
"The kingdom of heaven is like treasure hidden in a field. When a man found it, he hid it again, and then in his joy went and sold all he had and bought that field." Matthew 13:44

The parable of the hidden treasure

The man in this story gave up everything he owned for a hidden treasure. The treasure was far more valuable than any of the possessions the man sold. In the same way, we receive a treasure that is far more valuable than anything we have. That treasure is heaven. Jesus paid a great price to forgive our sins so we can go to heaven one day. He shed His blood for us. He gave His life on the cross to forgive our sin and rose again to give us new life. Those who believe in Jesus receive the treasures He offers—forgiveness, new life, eternal life, love, joy, and the like.

Bible Baseball

SUPPLIES
Pattern (right)
Card stock or poster board
Transparent tape
Marking pens
Index cards
1 coin, preferably a quarter

Directions

Before play begins, make a card stock cube using the pattern (enlarged to any size). Tape the sides of the cube with transparent tape. On three sides of the cube print the word "single." On one side each, print "double," "triple," and "home run." Have your students help you write twenty or more questions concerning the facts of the Bible stories you have studied. (For example, who is our Good Shepherd?) Print each question on an index card; print the answer on the reverse side. You, as the teacher, will ask the questions when play begins.

Divide the class into two teams. Let each team choose a team name. Print each name in a separate column on the chalkboard or large sheet of paper for score keeping. In your classroom or play area, designate home plate, first base, second base, and third base. Be sure each student knows where these places are.

Flip a coin to see which team goes first. The first "batter" stands at home plate. Read a question from the cards. If the student answers correctly, he or she rolls the cube to see how far he or she will proceed around the bases. The student then travels to that base and waits for the next person's turn. If the student rolls home run, he or she trots around the bases and sits back down with his or her teammates, scoring a run. Record runs on your scoreboard.

If players answer correctly and advance to a base, other players on base advance as well. If the batter answers incorrectly, it is recorded as one "out" for his team. A limit of five runs can be scored in one inning by a team. After three outs or five runs, the opposing team comes to bat.

This game provides a fun way for students to review Bible story facts. Be sure to divide teams according to ability so both teams have a chance to succeed.

Bible Connection

This activity can be used with any Bible story or verse. Consider using it with memory work for the week.

First Aid Relay

SUPPLIES

Large white cotton dishtowel tied to use as a sling
  (2 or more depending upon class size)
Long elastic bandages, 2 or more
Small adhesive bandages, 1 per person
Crutch or cane, 2 or more

Directions

Before play begins, mark off a 20-foot course. Establish a starting line.

Divide the class into two or more teams, four people per team. Have each team line up at the starting line. Give the first person on each team a sling, an elastic bandage, an adhesive bandage, and a crutch or cane.

When you say "Go," the first player on each team should slip his right arm into the sling, put the elastic bandage on his knee, stick the adhesive bandage on his left palm, and walk with the crutch or cane on the 20 foot long course and back to the starting line. Team members can help the participant put on and take off the props.

When the first player returns to the starting line, he gives each item (except the adhesive bandage) to the next person in line. This person follows the same procedure as described above. Be sure to give each new player a fresh adhesive bandage. The first team to have all players successfully complete the relay wins.

Bible Connection
As [Jesus] was going into a village, ten men who had leprosy met Him.
They stood at a distance and called out in a loud voice, "Jesus, Master,

have pity on us!" When He saw them, He said, "Go, show yourselves to the priests." And as they went, they were cleansed. Luke 17:12–14

Ten healed of leprosy

This Bible story is about God's grace and our response. In this short account, we are reminded that Jesus brings God's mercy to all people regardless of their social, physical, or regional condition. Luke doesn't tell us how the other nine react to the miraculous healing. What he does tell us is that only one of the men, a despised Samaritan, returns to Jesus with his thanks and praise: "[The healed man] came back, praising God in a loud voice. He threw himself at Jesus' feet, and thanked Him" (Luke 17:15–16). This Bible story teaches us that faith requires action. We are all fatally sick with sin. There is no hope of recovery except through the Word and work of Jesus Christ. Through the means of grace—God's Word and the Sacraments—we are cleansed of our sins and are given salvation. Our proper response is to return to Him with our thanks and praise.

Toilet Tissue Wrap Relay

SUPPLIES
2 rolls of toilet tissue (or more depending on class size)

Directions

Divide the class into two or more teams of four people each. Have each team stand close to one another in a circle, face out with their backs toward the center of the circle. Give one member of each team a roll of toilet tissue. When you say "Go," teammates are to unroll the tissue around themselves in the circle by handing the roll of paper from person to person around the circle. Teams should continue wrapping until the roll of tissue is empty. The first team to empty their roll of tissue in this manner is the winner.

Bible Connections
Jesus called in a loud voice, "Lazarus, come out!" The dead man came out, his hands and feet wrapped with strips of linen, and a cloth around his face. Jesus said to them, "Take off the grave clothes and let him go." John 11:43–44

Jesus raises Lazarus from the dead

The tissue wrapping recalls the wrapping of Lazarus in burial cloths. The story of Lazarus is about love and compassion—compassion for a friend and for Mary and Martha. Jesus wept at Lazarus's tomb because He understood what it's like to feel grief. He understands our sadness too and will always be there to comfort us. Remind students that Jesus truly does care about them and all their troubles. In fact, He loves them so much that He died on the cross for them. Still, that wasn't the end. Like Lazarus, Jesus rose from the dead. But Lazarus rose initially only to life on earth; Jesus rose to give us life with Him in heaven.

Tree Coin Toss

SUPPLIES
Coat tree
Brown wrapping paper or brown paper bags
Masking tape
Stapler and staples (optional)
4 small lightweight baskets with handles
4 lightweight plastic caps from gallon milk jugs

Directions

Cover a coat tree with brown wrapping paper to make it look like a real tree. Twist and crinkle long pieces of the paper and tape or staple them to the coat tree to form several long branches. Hang the four baskets at various places on the tree by putting the basket handles over the tree "limbs." Be sure to place one basket in an easy-to-reach place to help make play successful for all students. Make a masking-tape line on the floor about 8 feet in front of the tree. Have the students line up at this masking-tape line. Give the first child in line the four plastic milk jug caps, representing Zacchaeus's coins. Keeping their toes behind the line, the students are to toss the caps into the tree baskets. Each student receives one point for each cap that lands and stays in a basket. After four tries, collect the milk caps and give them to the next student in line.

Options: Older students may enjoy playing this game in teams where a team's total points are added together. You could also assign various point values to the baskets in the tree (e.g., the higher in the tree the basket is, the greater the number of points that are awarded if a cap lands in it).

Bible Connection
Jesus said to [Zacchaeus], "Today salvation has come to this house, because this man, too, is a son of Abraham. For the Son of Man came to seek and to save what was lost." Luke 19:9–10

Zacchaeus the tax collector

Work as a tax collector for the hated Romans made Zacchaeus a pariah to the people and excluded him from the synagogue and temple. Jesus' loving acceptance changed Zacchaeus. Zacchaeus demonstrated his new faith by helping the poor and

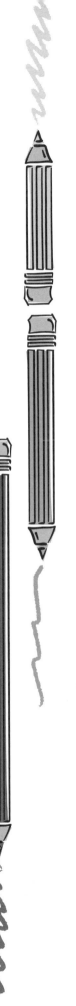

repaying those he cheated. God's unconditional love in Jesus changes our hearts, minds, and spirits too. He fills us with love and hope and changes us from selfish, self-centered people to children of God who serve Him with joy.

Use this game as a recreational activity in connection with the Bible story of Zacchaeus. Encourage the students to cheer for one another as points are scored. Students waiting in line to play the game could sing "Zacchaeus."

Wash Away Sins

SUPPLIES
1 squirt gun
1 bucket of water (optional)
8" x 12" portable whiteboard
Water soluble markers

Directions

Fill squirt guns. Define a starting line. Mark another line about 20 feet away.

Divide class into teams. Give one whiteboard and marker to each team. Have each team select someone to write a list of sins on the board. Discuss sin with the students, its consequences, and how God saved us from sin through His Son, Jesus. Give teams about two minutes to list at least ten sins, such as lying, cheating, stealing, and so forth. After two minutes, the volunteer stands behind the other line holding the whiteboard. The rest of the team waits behind the starting line. Each player will run to the board and squirt the board until one sin word disappears. If you run out of words before everyone has a chance to play, write more on the board. If time allows, keep writing words and let kids have more than one turn.

Options: Write sins with chalk on a sidewalk or parking lot. (It's harder to wash away.) For younger children, shorten the distance to the whiteboard.

Bible Connection
Wash away all my iniquity and cleanse me from my sin. Psalm 51:2

Jesus washes away our sin

It takes real courage and strength to follow God's will and God's ways. Thankfully, we are not on our own; God is with us. He has redeemed us through the power of Christ Jesus and transforms our lives through the empowering of the Holy Spirit.

Forgiving or washing away sins is impossible by ourselves. Nothing we can do makes sin go away. But the Bible says that those who believe in Jesus receive the forgiveness of sins that He obtained for us. Jesus never sinned, but He took our sins on Himself when He died on the cross. When Jesus forgives our sins, they are truly washed away!

Get-Me-Wet Shipwreck

SUPPLIES
Small pieces of paper
Pen or marker
1 bucket of water
2 sponges

Directions

Depending on class size, make two sets of numbered pieces of paper. You need two people in the class with the same number. Toss sponges in bucket of water.

Have the class sit in a circle, at least an arm's length away from their neighbors. Put the bucket in the middle of the circle. Give every person a number. Call out a number. Whoever has the number must get up and run around the circle. When they get back to their place, they should run into the circle, grab a sponge from the bucket, and throw it at the other person. Continue play until everyone has had a chance to play.

Option: For younger children, use foam balls instead of sponges.

Bible Connection
I can do everything through Him who gives me strength.
Philippians 4:13

Paul's shipwreck

Paul faced some dangerous situations. He was imprisoned, threatened, and experienced a terrible storm that wrecked the ship he was on. Certainly the days seemed grim, but Paul had the riches of God's grace in Christ Jesus. He believed in Jesus and spent his life telling others about his Savior. God saved him and all those aboard, but everyone got wet, just like you did.

Jesus loved Paul and was with him in good and bad times. He wouldn't abandon Paul. In fact, God preserved Paul so he could testify before Caesar and he continued to testify about Christ. Jesus loves us too. He died and rose from the dead to set us free from sin and give us a rich relationship with Him, now and forever. He is with us in good and bad times. He gives us opportunities to tell others about Him. God be with you as you do so today.

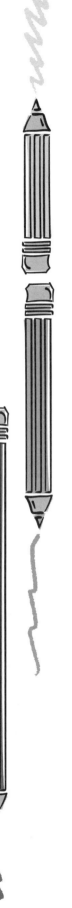

Bubblelympics

SUPPLIES
Individual bottles of nontoxic bubble fluid and small wands
Hula Hoop
A stopwatch or wristwatch with a second hand

Directions

Divide the class into pairs. Give each student his or her own bottle of bubble fluid and a small wand. Let each pair work together in the following bubble competitions:

Hit the target. See how many bubbles they can blow in thirty seconds. The bubbles are to land inside the area enclosed by the hoop or garden hose.

Chain-link bubbles. Have one person from each pair blow a bubble that remains on the tip of the bubble wand. That person's partner tries to blow a bubble and try to connect it to the first bubble without breaking either one. Let other teams join the challenge to see how many bubbles can be joined together in a chain.

Bubble high jump. Have both members of each pair blow a bubble upward at the same time. Time how long each stays afloat and unbroken.

Megabubbles. Have a friendly competition among class members as to who can blow the largest bubble. Cheer the winner!

Bible Connection
Since we are surrounded by such a great cloud of witnesses, let us
throw off everything that hinders and the sin that so easily entangles,
and let us run with perseverance the race marked out for us.
Hebrews 12:1

The communion of saints

The Holy Spirit uses visible tools like God's Word, the waters of Holy Baptism, and the bread and wine/body and blood of Christ in Communion to create and sustain faith. Through them, we are able to believe, the forgiveness of sins becomes ours, and we are enabled to live as God's children. The Holy Spirit connects sinners with Jesus and the sinners become saints, children of God. The same Spirit keeps believers in the faith, strengthens their faith through the activities of the church, and assures them how the truths we cannot see—like the forgiveness of sins, the resurrection of the bodies of believers on the Last Day to live in the next life—are real and certain. As you use these bubble activities, thank God together with your students for the joy He gives you in Jesus.

Scripture Index

Scripture Verse	Bible Story	Activity	Page
Genesis 1:1	Creation	Creation Walk	6
Genesis 1:16–18	The fourth day of creation	Sun, Moon, and Stars	49
Genesis 1:31	Creation	Creation Scramble	43
Genesis 3:1	The fall of man	Get That Snake	46
Genesis 3:14–15	God promises a Savior	Watch the Snake!	39
Genesis 6:11–13, 18	The flood	Hammer It	7
Genesis 14–16	The flood	Pair Up	12
Exodus 8:1–2	Moses and the ten plagues	Leap Frog	20
Exodus 12:31–32	The exodus	Journey Time Relay	54
Exodus 15:1	The song of Moses' thanksgiving	Thanksgiving Roll	10
Exodus 34:28	The Ten Commandments	Can You Guess It?	34
Joshua 2:8–12	Rahab and the spies	Winning Together, Working Together	40
1 Samuel 3:21	The Lord calls Samuel	Decoder Wheel	13
1 Samuel 17:40	David and Goliath	Smooth Stones Tick-Tac-Toe	19
1 Samuel 17:45	David and Goliath	Giant Beanbag Throw	32
1 Samuel 20:42	David and Jonathan	Friendship Challenges	45
Psalm 23:1–3	The Lord is my Shepherd	Magnetic Maze	17
Psalm 51:2	Jesus washes away our sin	Wash Away Sins	60
Matthew 2:2	The visit of the Magi	Look Up and Go!	48
Matthew 2:9–10	The visit of the Magi	Follow-the-Star Game	28
Matthew 2:13–18	The escape to Egypt	Faithful Followers	44
Matthew 4:18–20	The calling of the first disciples	Follow Me!	6
Matthew 6:25–26, 33	Do not worry	Jesus Loves Me	33
Matthew 7:7–8	The Lord's Prayer	Pop-a-Prayer Pal	8
Matthew 7:24–25	The wise and foolish builders	Builders' Challenge	36
Matthew 9:37–38	The workers are few	Bring-in-the-Harvest Game	24
Matthew 13:44	The parable of the hidden treasure	Treasure Rescue	55
Mark 2:3–5	Jesus heals the paralyzed man	Mat Mayhem	53
Mark 9:35	Who is the greatest?	Pebble Search	22
Luke 5:10–11	Fishers of men	Fishing for Men	45
Luke 15:1–7	The parable of the lost sheep	Magnetic Maze	17
Luke 17:12–14	Ten healed of leprosy	First Aid Relay	57
Luke 19:3–4	Zacchaeus the tax collector	Tree Tag	49
Luke 19:9–10	Zacchaeus the tax collector	Tree Coin Toss	59
Luke 19:10	The parable of the lost sheep	Gather-the-Flock Game	16
Luke 23:26	The crucifixion	Challenge Walk	42

Reference	Topic	Activity	Page
Luke 24:30–32	On the road to Emmaus	Disappearing Act	10
John 1:40–42	Jesus' first disciples	Fishing Game	38
John 6:8–9	Jesus feeds the 5,000	Basket, Fish, and Bread	35
John 11:43–44	Jesus raises Lazarus from the dead	Toilet Tissue Wrap Relay	58
John 14:2	Jesus comforts His disciples	Mansion Checkers	21
John 20:29	Jesus appears to Thomas	Faith Hurdles	50
John 21:6	The miraculous catch of fish	"Catch a Fish" Game	31
Acts 1:8	Share the Good News about Jesus	Tic-Tac-Tell Game	23
Acts 1:9	Jesus ascends to heaven	Up Ball	51
Acts 8:30–31	Philip and the Ethiopian	Horse Course	40
1 Corinthians 9:24–25	The best prize	Game Sticks	15
Galatians 5:16	Life by the Spirit	"Forgiven Sins" Memory Game	25
Philippians 4:13	Paul's shipwreck	Get-Me-Wet Shipwreck	61
Hebrews 4:15	Jesus, our high Priest	Human Confusion	11
Hebrews 11:30	The fall of Jericho	Demolished but Rebuilt	37
Hebrews 12:1	The communion of saints	Bubblelympics	62
Hebrews 12:2	Staying focused	Hit or Miss	47